The Book of
Basketball Wisdom

The Book of
Basketball Wisdom

Common Sense and Uncommon Genius
From 101 Basketball Greats

Compiled and Edited by Criswell Freeman

WALNUT GROVE PRESS
Nashville, TN 37205

ISBN 1-887655-32-8

The ideas expressed in this book are not, in all cases, exact quotations, as some have been edited for clarity and brevity. In all cases, the author has attempted to maintain the speaker's original intent. In some cases, material for this book was obtained from secondary sources, primarily print media. While every effort was made to ensure the accuracy of these sources, the accuracy cannot be guaranteed. For additions, deletions, corrections or clarifications in future editions of this text, please write WALNUT GROVE PRESS.

Printed in the United States of America
Cover Design by Mary Mazer
Typesetting & Page Layout by Sue Gerdes
Editor for Walnut Grove Press: Alan Ross
2 3 4 5 6 7 8 9 10   98 99 00 01

ACKNOWLEDGMENTS
The author gratefully acknowledges the helpful support of Angela Beasley, Dick and Mary Freeman, and Mary Susan Freeman.

For Jamie Tillman

Head Coach of the Green Hornets, 1967

Table of Contents

Introduction

In 1891, Luther H. Gulick, the director of the YMCA Training School in Springfield, Massachusetts summoned one of his part-time instructors, an energetic young man named James Naismith. Gulick asked Naismith to develop an indoor sport that would occupy students during the cold New England winters. So Naismith invented basketball.

For over a century, Naismith's game has produced an entertaining collection of coaches and players, icons and rogues. This book serves as a concise collection of their collective genius.

Anyone who has ever enjoyed a slam duck or a rainbow three-pointer owes a lasting debt to James Naismith. He's the fellow who hung up that first peach basket and got the ball rolling (or, more precisely, bouncing). Without Naismith, there would have been no epic battles between Chamberlain and Russell. And we would have missed that magic rivalry between Bird and Johnson. Pete Maravich would have been an anonymous lanky kid with droopy socks. And Hakeem Olajuwon would have been the world's tallest soccer goalie. Absent Dr. Naismith, we would have missed March Madness, the Final Four, and the NBA Playoffs. And Michael Jordan might have been a light-hitting minor league outfielder.

Happily, Naismith invented a game that has allowed some of history's greatest athletes to showcase their skills. Hopefully, this book will showcase their wisdom.

1

All-Purpose Advice

Long before the first ball was dribbled or the first sneaker was laced, Sophocles wrote, "No enemy is worse than bad advice." Twenty-five centuries later, basketball coaches took up the search for the kind of advice that would win games and improve lives. Chuck Daly once noted, "Coaching is still more art than science." The same could be said for the all-purpose advice on the following pages.

Make each day your masterpiece.

John Wooden

My father taught me this:
Do the right thing, never forget your roots,
and always count your blessings.

Shaquille O'Neal

Talent is God-given; be humble.
Fame is man-given; be thankful.
Conceit is self-given; be careful.

John Wooden

Stay hungry,
stay humble.

Hakeem Olajuwon

Act quickly, but don't hurry.

John Wooden

Think and then act.
Never act and then alibi.

Hank Iba

Keep it simple.
When you get too complicated,
you forget the obvious.

Al McGuire

Since there are no secrets, keep it simple.

Dale Brown

Show me a guy who can't say "no" and I'll show you a guy with problems, lots of problems.

Red Auerbach

Never worry about criticism from the misinformed.

Adolph Rupp

If you isolate your problem from others,
your chances of solving it are thin.
Problems require wisdom, and wisdom
requires perspective. Other people
provide that perspective.

Bill Russell

Destruction isn't necessarily a bad thing;
it can be good if what you're destroying is
immaturity, the fear of failure, jealousy
or lack of commitment.

Mike Krzyzewski

The player or coach with superior talent
should be willing to take some risks.

Bob Cousy

The best thing you can do is
be your own person.

Larry Bird

Don't let what you cannot do interfere with
what you can do.

John Wooden

My advice to kids?
Don't be like me — be better than me.

Shaquille O'Neal

Always keep an open mind and a compassionate heart.

Phil Jackson

2

Attitude

Adolph Rupp was a coach with an attitude. The crusty boss of the Kentucky Wildcats claimed, "Every boy who puts on a Kentucky uniform just plays a little better than he would in one of another color." His confidence was contagious. Frank Ramsey observed, "Coach Rupp convinced us that we could do things we didn't know we could do."

Adolph Rupp was correct about the power of a proper mental attitude, but he didn't go far enough. The self-fulfilling prophecy doesn't only apply in Kentucky; it is alive and well on basketball courts everywhere.

Winning is an attitude.

John Chaney

Conceive the inconceivable —
then accomplish it.

Jim Valvano

Refuse to lose.

John Calipari's Favorite Slogan

Spirit is contagious.

Adolph Rupp

To me, it's a serious game.
Don't expect me to be havin' all kinds of fun
when the score's tied, two seconds are left,
and the other guys have the ball.

Larry Bird

Any game we're down even 10 points going
into the fourth quarter we can still win.

Willis Reed

There's no one else in the world I want
to have the ball for the last shot but me.

Larry Bird

Never fear, E. J. is here.

Magic Johnson

We're not out to physically harm them,
but I wouldn't mind hurting their feelings.

Kareem Abdul-Jabbar

Obviously there have been times when
I've failed. But there have never been times
when I thought I would fail.

Michael Jordan

Shooting is nothing. Anybody can shoot.
The big thrill is putting on a show
for the crowd.

Pete Maravich

To be an innovator, you can't be worried
about making mistakes.

Julius Erving

I can't stand a ballplayer who plays in fear.

Red Auerbach

Confidence means being able
to laugh at yourself.

Bill Russell

Play the game with a smile.

Earl "The Pearl" Monroe

Ambition is okay as long as you can control it.
When it starts controlling you,
you've got problems.

Red Auerbach

Great effort springs naturally
from a great attitude.

Pat Riley

I will not let anything get in the way of me
and my competitive enthusiasm to win.

Michael Jordan

Believe in yourself, your players and
your system of play.

Jerry Tarkanian

You can't afford negative thinking,
so you always believe you will win. You build
an image of yourself that has nothing to do
with ego, but it has to be satisfied.

Bob Pettit

Believe in yourself. If you believe
you can do something, don't let anybody
in the whole world tell you you can't.

Slick Watts

I felt there was no one in the league
who could stop me if I was playing hard.

Larry Bird

When I'm on my game, I don't think there's
anybody who can stop me.

Michael Jordan

One thing I don't believe in: excuses.

Karl Malone

I don't look for excuses when we lose,
and I don't buy excuses when we win.

Dave Cowens

The most important quality I look for
in a player is accountability. You've got to be
accountable for who you are. It's too easy
to blame things on someone else.

Lenny Wilkens

A man may make mistakes,
but he isn't a failure until he starts
blaming someone else.

John Wooden

Blame is the coward's way out.

Elvin Hayes

You have to expect things of yourself
before you can do them.

Michael Jordan

Complacency is an ugly monster
that sneaks up behind us, trips us,
and makes us fall short of our goals.

Dale Brown

For every peak, there's a valley,
so don't get too high.

John Wooden

The difference between a winner and a loser is a matter of inches — and a matter of attitude.

Nancy Lieberman

The mental approach to things is what separates players at every level.

Lisa Leslie

We are not going to play them; they are going to play us.

Hank Iba

I don't think you can teach desire. I think it's a gift.

Larry Bird

Where do you find motivation? You find it within yourself.

Michael Jordan

Be a dreamer. If you don't know how to dream, you're dead.

Jim Valvano

3

Life

Friedrich Nietzsche wrote, "The most instructive experiences are those of everyday life." Nietzsche, a 19th century German philosopher, knew nothing about basketball, but his words still apply to the everyday world of hoops. The game demands discipline, preparation and mental toughness; lessons of the hardwood apply inside the gym or out.

Coach Ray Meyer once observed, "Basketball is a slice of life. There is good in every experience if you learn from it." On the following pages, we learn about life from some of basketball's greatest legends. Nietzche would be proud.

I learned early that if I wanted to achieve
anything in life, I'd have to do it myself.
I learned that I had to be accountable.

Lenny Wilkens

Whatever formula you apply to your life
should be the one that enables you
to maintain consistency.

Julius Erving

Everyone should want to excel in life.
You should never take the desire to excel
away from the human race.

Hank Iba

Always focus on what you want to achieve.

Michael Jordan

My message is simple:
Take control of your life.

Charles Barkley

It doesn't make sense to be nervous
    playing basketball. There are too many
    other things in life to be nervous about.

Jalen Rose

The most important thing in a person's life
    is his faith and how he translates his faith
    into practical deeds.

Hakeem Olajuwon

When you remember God,
    God remembers you.

Hakeem Olajuwon

Live in the precious present.

Rick Pitino

Everybody who tries to accomplish
    something big takes the chance
    of a big disappointment.

John Thompson

Everyone is born with a certain potential.
You may never achieve your full potential, but
how close you come depends on how much
    you want to pay the price.

Red Auerbach

Don't measure yourself by what
    you have accomplished but by what you
should have accomplished with your ability.

John Wooden

The dream comes true
    when you reach your potential.

John Calipari

Be the dream.

John Chaney

It takes education to be successful
in the game of life.

Bob Lanier

The bottom line — no matter where you
come from or your economic background —
is to associate yourself with people
interested in making your life better.

Grant Hill

Once you get a taste
of where you want to go,
motivation takes care
of itself.

Chuck Daly

Be strong in body, clean in mind, lofty in ideals.

James Naismith

4

Practice

Basketball skills are not learned overnight. Countless hours of practice are required. Bobby Knight observed, "The will to win is grossly overrated. The will to prepare is far more important." Coach Knight understood that champions are made on the practice court.

Behind every great player, there is a story of tireless effort in pursuit of basketball excellence. Whether it's the neighborhood gym, the backyard goal or the urban playground, court fanatics find a way to play. And sometimes, practice makes perfect.

Many, many times, the kids with less talent
become the better athletes because
they're more dedicated to achieving
their full potential.

Red Auerbach

If you want a view from the top, practice,
not parties, will take you where
you want to go.

Kevin Johnson

More depth, more options,
great competition in practice — these things
make you a better team.

Mike Krzyzewski

I am not a strategic coach;
I am a practice coach.

John Wooden

Any team can be a miracle team, but you have to go out and work for your miracles.

Pat Riley

First, master the fundamentals.

Larry Bird

Opponents will always find your weakness
and it doesn't take long. Weaknesses stand
out like a neon sign. So don't just practice
your strengths. Practice your weaknesses.

Magic Johnson

Failure to prepare is preparing to fail.

John Wooden

The number one thing is desire,
   the ability to do the things you have to do
      to become a basketball player.

Larry Bird

The only way to find your rhythm
is by repetition. Do a thing a thousand times
     and pretty soon you do it easily
       and gracefully.

Adolph Rupp

I want my players to save their energy
      for the game.

John Wooden

Oned day of practice
is like one day of clean
living. It doesn't do you
any good.

Abe Lemons

5

Court Smarts

All basketball players are not created equal. Some possess an almost magical ability to see the court and understand the flow of the game. When this talent is nurtured through years of practice, a sixth sense evolves. The names are legend: Cousy, Robertson, Johnson, Bird, Maravich, Monroe, and Stockton, to name but a few.

One such player was Isiah Thomas, a point guard who combined limitless talent with a gritty determination to win. For Isiah, the court was his means of expression. He once said, "There's nothing quite like the feeling of being inside those four lines and doing your thing." And for those of us who witness true basketball wizardry, there's nothing quite like watching the show.

Look at the teams that had the great years. It's the ones that had the guards who could penetrate, break down the defense, and then move the ball to the right people.

Kevin McHale

Play to win. You can't play tentatively; you can't play scared.

Rollie Massimino

Great teams develop total communication on the floor. Basketball intellects mesh perfectly. They never have to call a play.

John Havlicek

The best way to get your players to do what you want is to make them coaches on the court.

Don Meyer

You can't teach court savvy.

Dean Smith

It don't matter who scores the points.
It's who gets the ball to the scorer.

Larry Bird

This may sound funny, but shooting isn't
my game. Passing is.

Pete Maravich

Anticipation is the name of the game
        for a little backcourt man.

Slick Watts

When you move without the ball,
        good things happen.

Bill Walton

You got to get the ball before you
        can shoot it.

Moses Malone

I couldn't run, and I couldn't jump so I tried
    to become a great shooter and passer.

Larry Bird

I'm not against taking shots, but I am against taking bad shots.

Hank Iba

Basketball is like a really fast-paced
game of chess, where every move has
its benefits and repercussions.
Bill Walton

Basketball is like a game of chess.
But until you win the championship,
it's not checkmate.
Isiah Thomas

6

Teamwork

The game of basketball provides a wonderful showcase for individual athletic ability. But consistent winning depends more upon teamwork that upon the singular talents of any one player. Wilt Chamberlain, the most dominant center of his era, was thwarted again and again by the precision teamwork of the Boston Celtics. Even the limitless talents of Michael Jordan were simply not enough to bring home the NBA hardware until his supporting cast provided sufficient support.

Red Auerbach said this about team play: "Some people believe you win with your five best players, but I found out that you win with the five who fit together best." Well said, Red.

Generally speaking, individual performances
don't win basketball games.

John Wooden

The greatest players fit with the team.
They play within the team's style, rather than
asking the team to change its style.

Patrick Ewing

Once a player becomes bigger than
the team, you no longer have a team.

Red Auerbach

We play as a team. One-man teams
are losing teams.

Kareem Abdul-Jabbar

Winning is about having the whole team on the same page.

Bill Walton

The nicest thing people ever said about me
as a basketball player was that I made the
players around me better. To me,
there's no higher compliment.

Bill Walton

To me, a great player is someone who gives
it all he's got and makes the players
around him better.

Karl Malone

It's not my job to look good. It's my job
to make other people look good.

Wes Unseld

The MVP depends on what you do for
your team, what you do to make
everybody else play better, and above all,
whether or not you win.

Isiah Thomas

Our goal is not to win. It's to play together and play hard. Then, winning takes care of itself.

Mike Krzyzewski

In basketball, personal goals have little meaning. Team goals are the only ones that really matter.

Jack Ramsay

Individual honors are nice, but victory belongs to the team.

Red Auerbach

We have a lot of leaders.
They put their egos on hold.
Jack McCloskey

There's nothing like respect on a basketball
team — toward the coach,
toward one another.
Lenny Wilkens

I played terrible basketball in the '72 Finals.
And we won. I was playing so poorly that the
team overcame me. Maybe that's what being
a team is all about.
Jerry West

The final test of a championship team is how
strongly the players believe in each other.
Chuck Daly

The team itself must be the leader of the team.

Phil Jackson

Sometimes a player's greatest challenge
is coming to grips with his role on the team.

Scottie Pippen

Molding a team begins with
a clear definition of each player's role.

Jack Ramsay

There are people with a lot more talent
than I have who have been weeded out
of the league because they couldn't
put their egos aside to fill a role.

Kurt Rambis

A great team is like a Swiss watch —
a bunch of moving parts working together.

Jo Jo White

You're not going to win with the kids who are just All-Americans. The kids must have more than status, they must have togetherness.

John Thompson

It's amazing how much can be accomplished if no one cares who gets the credit.

John Wooden

Eliminate team jealousy.

Al McGuire

People think teamwork is some mysterious
force. It can really be manufactured
by serving each player's needs.

Bill Russell

The best teams have chemistry.
They communicate with each other and they
sacrifice personal glory for a common goal.

Dave DeBusschere

I still say the most important thing
in winning basketball games is chemistry.

Shawn Kemp

Victory never belongs to the individual.
Victory belongs to the team.

Red Auerbach

Great teamwork is the only way we create
the breakthroughs that define our careers.

Pat Riley

If you go out with one focus in mind,
to contribute to the team's success,
individual accolades will take care
of themselves.

Michael Jordan

Play as a team and eliminate all thoughts of personal glory.

Claire Bee

7

Hard Work

The greatest basketball players make the near-impossible look easy. But the gift of greatness has a price, and that price is hard work. In this regard, no apostle of the game was more vocal than John Wooden. He once proclaimed, "My definition of success is peace of mind obtained by doing the best you can to be the best you are."

In this chapter, we consider the manifold virtues of a hard day's work. Whether you're an all-star on the court, in the school room, at the office, or in the home, the price of victory is consistent effort. The following basketball legends became legends only after years of training. As they will staunchly attest, work works.

Winners aren't built overnight.

Bill Fitch

I don't care whether we win or lose,
just as long as we work hard.

Charles Barkley

Win, lose or draw, the work itself
is what really counts.

Julius Erving

If I work hard enough, we win.

Isiah Thomas

When the stars work hard, you've got it
made because the other players feel foolish
if they're not working.

John Wooden

Nothing will work unless you do.

John Wooden

Nothing is work unless
you'd rather be doing
something else.

Dick Motta

Hard Work

My vision, my court awareness and
　　my height are God-given. Everything else
　　　　I worked my butt off for.

Larry Bird

What I put into my basketball
　　　　is what I get out of it.

Grant Hill

They say good things come to those
　　who wait. I believe good things come
　　　　to those who work.

Wilt Chamberlain

It's not how good you are.
　　　　It's how good you can be.

Kevin McHale

Work is a good word. When we work hard at something we enjoy and feel good about, we feel good about ourselves again and again and again.

Mike Krzyzewski

The best players, when they detect a weakness in their own game, go out and work on it until the weakness becomes a strength.

Bill Walton

If you play hard every night, the fans will be in your corner. That's what we're all working toward.

Pat Riley

There are times when you struggle. But the important thing is this: Keep your effort constant.

Kareem Abdul-Jabbar

Idleness breeds mischief.

James Naismith's Motto

You can't get much done
in life if you only work
on the days when
you feel good.

Jerry West

The problem with doing nothing is that you never know when you're through.

Wilt Chamberlain

8

Success

General Douglas MacArthur warned, "It is fatal to enter any war without the will to win it." The same principle applies to battles on the hardwood. Basketball is a war of wills. The team that learns to maintain its concentration throughout the entire game is destined for success. Without the will to win, even a talented squad will falter.

Once a team learns to summon its collective willpower, victory becomes habit-forming. One win leads to another, and then another. Finally, the team's confidence level becomes its greatest asset. As Adolph Rupp correctly observed, "Success is the glue that holds a great team together."

Here, we consider proven prescriptions for success. Like the admonitions of General MacArthur and The Baron, these words apply on the court or off.

You have to have ability, but ability alone
is not enough.

John Thompson

Trying to get by on talent is a fatal mistake.

Pete Maravich

You can win and still not succeed,
still not achieve what you should. And you
can lose without really failing at all.

Bobby Knight

Doing the best you are capable of doing
is victory in itself, and less than that
is defeat.

John Wooden

You're not always going
to be successful, but if
you're afraid to fail,
you don't deserve
to be successful.

Charles Barkley

Championship rings, I live for them.

Larry Bird

I don't think I'm a better coach now that we've won the national championship.

Dean Smith

I only know how to play two ways. That's reckless and abandon.

Magic Johnson

If you can play, you can play; if you can't, you can't. No matter how tall, short, skinny or fat someone is, you can't measure athletic ability or a person's heart.

Charles Barkley

.

Money is only part of the dream.
The dream is to be whatever you set out to be
— to fulfill your potential.

Red Auerbach

Don't let other people tell you
what you want out of life.

Pat Riley

The great teams learn how to win
night after night, week after week,
season after season, with no letup.

Don Nelson

Coaches don't win championships.
Administrations win championships.

John Calipari

I was nervous all the time.
That's where I got my energy.

Jerry West

Sometimes, adrenaline flows
into momentum.

Dennis Johnson

A lot of days you just want to give up,
but the hard work and the pressure
make a better man out of you.
It prepares you for life.

Jack Givens

To be successful, you have to like to lose
a little less than everybody else.

Phil Jackson

Success is the best character builder.

Adolph Rupp

Success comes from talent, hard work
and luck.

Kareem Abdul-Jabbar

Basketball is a game of habits.

John Wooden

Beauty is just like a player's statistics.
Neither one tells the real story.

Red Auerbach

Leadership is diving after loose balls.

Larry Bird

What's the secret of surviving in the NBA? Patience.

Robert Parish

Success is never final.
Failure is never fatal.
It's courage that counts.

John Wooden

9

Defense and Rebounding

The great irony of basketball is this: Offense makes headlines, but defense and rebounding win championships. As Dr. Jack Ramsay correctly observed, "Victory is always within reach of a strong defensive team." The same could be said for relentless rebounders.

During his heyday, there was no better board man than Moses Malone. In 1983, Malone topped the NBA in rebounding while leading his Philadelphia 76ers to the league championship. With his tireless work on the offensive boards, he earned Most Valuable Player status. But more importantly, Moses won the hard-earned respect of his peers while proving once and for all that, in basketball, rebounding is the way to the promised land.

A team's defense is
the foremost part of its
overall game plan.
Defense, in a word,
is dominant.

Jack Ramsay

Defense is the foundation and heart
of the game of basketball.

Jerry Tarkanian

Defense is just hard work. There will be
nights when your shots won't fall, but
you can play good defense every night.

Red Auerbach

You don't have to be "on" to play defense.
We hang our hat on defense.

Chuck Daly

Defense will save you on the nights
when your offense isn't working.

Adolph Rupp

Russell's first law:
You must make the other
player do what you
want him to do.

Bill Russell

I want us to play
mother-in-law defense:
constant nagging
and harassment.

Rick Pitino

I really believe defense is an art.

Dennis Johnson

I'd rather block a shot than score.

Bill Russell

The idea is not to block every shot.
The idea is to make your opponent believe
that you might block every shot.

Bill Russell

You've got to hate being embarrassed
on defense.

Isiah Thomas

One way to regain your rhythm on offense
is to make some big plays on defense.
Bill Walton

The team with a great defense coupled with
a good offense will almost always defeat the
team with a good defense and a great offense.
Phog Allen

I stress offense without the ball and defense
before the other player gets the ball.
John Wooden

Wooden's Bruins stripped and dismantled
taller opponents like a band of LA car thieves
working over a parked car.
Billy Packer

All great teams have two things in common:
defense and rebounding.

Larry Brown

Rebounding is not about how tall you are
or how high you jump, it's about positioning
and quickness.

Bill Walton

There is no glory in rebounding —
just victory.

George Raveling

If you can rebound, you can win.

Jerry West

I played against a lot of guys who could jump.
But they all came down.

Bob Hansen

I've scored 20,000 points,
but the thing I'm most
proud of in my career
is my rebounding.

Charles Barkley

Offense sells tickets.
Defense wins games.
Rebounds win
championships.

Pat Head Summitt

10

Coaching

The first true basketball coach was Forrest C. "Phog" Allen of the University of Kansas. Allen's mentor, Dr. James Naismith, invented the game but believed it too spontaneous for proper coaching. When Phog informed Naismith of plans to become a full-time basketball coach, the doubting doctor replied, "Forrest, you don't coach this game, you just play it."

Naismith was profoundly mistaken about the role of coaching in basketball. In this chapter, the game's greatest generals discuss the art of leadership. Because there's more to playing basketball than just playing.

Develop your coaching philosophy
   to complement your own personality.

Jerry Tarkanian

Determining his philosophy is a coach's
   primary task. He must decide, before
   anything else, what he wants to say
   of himself through his game.

Jack Ramsay

Coaches must change, but the underlying
   philosophy of the coach must remain
   the same.

John Wooden

I am the leader of my team. I know
   how to win. The players will do it my way,
   or they won't do it for me.

Adolph Rupp

Be yourself and don't imitate anyone
regardless of his success. The two most
successful coaches in the history of college
basketball, John Wooden and Adolph Rupp,
had completely opposite personalities.
So coach within your own makeup
and be yourself.

Dale Brown

A coach, to do his best job,
must be himself.

John Bunn

Awareness of one's personal philosophy
brings order and understanding
to the coaching process.

Jerry Tarkanian

A coach must be sold on himself.

Tex Winter

Coaching

Good coaching may be defined as the
development of character, personality
and habits of players, plus the teaching
of fundamentals and team play.

Claire Bee

Find players you can teach
and patterns they can run.

Jerry Tarkanian

The coach is first of all a teacher.

John Wooden

I've had 16 coaches in my life, and each one
of them taught me different lessons about life.

Pat Riley

It's not what you tell
them — it's what
they hear.

Red Auerbach

Good coaching begins with self-security.

Jack Ramsay

Coaching is classically a personality
transference to a ballclub.

Phil Jackson

Coaching is a means of self-expression.
Successful coaches, like artists,
have a characteristic style.

Jack Ramsay

We have certain ways of behaving on
this team. I'm not on their team —
they're playing on mine.

John Thompson

You can communicate without motivating, but it is impossible to motivate without communicating.

John Thompson

You must have a system, a way of doing
things, that you believe is sound.

John Thompson

The coach should be the absolute boss,
but he still should maintain an open mind.

Red Auerbach

As a coach, I may not always be liked,
but respect of my players is critical.

Don Nelson

Nobody talks back to me.

Adolph Rupp

If a coach starts listening to the fans, he winds up sitting next to them.

Johnny Kerr

In the old days, the name of the game
was coaching. Today, it's recruiting.

Hank Iba

There are four Ps of college coaching:
program, philosophy, personnel, and patterns.

Jerry Tarkanian

What I enjoy about basketball is the process,
the way things come together as you build
a winning program.

Willis Reed

It's easy to find great players. What's hard
is getting people to play as a team.
That's the selling job.

Chuck Daly

A coach can't afford to get too excited because his players will get excited, too. And then they won't be able to think clearly.

John McLendon, Jr.

There's far more overcoaching than undercoaching.

John Wooden

I never had a lot of rules, just a few important ones.

Red Auerbach

Keep mediocre talent on a tight rein. Unleash superior talent, and let it run.

Bob Cousy

A lot of guys go through their whole
coaching careers and don't win any
championships, but they're great coaches.

Chuck Daly

When a coach gets voted into the
Hall of Fame, the honor really belongs
to all those who played for him.

Bobby Knight

I learned a big secret in basketball a long, long time ago. Somebody has to be in charge.

Red Auerbach

Other people go to an
office. I get to coach.
I know I've been blessed.

Jim Valvano

11

Character

In 1898, Dr. Luther Gulick made this proclamation: "When men commence to make money out of sport, it degenerates with tremendous speed. It has inevitably resulted in men of lower character going into the game." If Luther Gulick thought sports earnings were out of control in 1898, think how he would feel about today's professional payrolls.

Contrary to Dr. Gulick's prediction, the game of basketball was not taken over by ruffians or thugs. Instead, the intervening century has produced countless coaches and players of high moral standing. From high school to the NBA, coaching and playing have proven to be honored professions. Meanwhile, tens of thousands of students have attended college on basketball scholarships. And the game has done much to promote understanding and good will among people of many diverse backgrounds. All of which proves that Dr. Gulick was a better academician than he was prognosticator.

Every game, every night,
    I did the best I could.

Julius Erving

Basketball was never a recreation for me.
It was my whole life — something I fell
        in love with.

Larry Bird

All great players are self motivated.

Kevin McHale

The only lasting form
of discipline is
self-imposed discipline.

Dale Brown

It's not up to anyone else to make me give my best.

Hakeem Olajuwon

To find the unlimited scope of human possibility, look within yourself.

Jim Valvano

You go along in life and work hard.
You reach new levels of accomplishment. And
with each level you reach, the demands upon
you become greater. Your pride increases to
meet the demands. You drive yourself
harder than before.

Bob Pettit

Be more concerned with your character
than your reputation. Your character is what
you really are, while your reputation is merely
what others think you are.

John Wooden

Character takes you just so far.
Then you've got to have talent.

Karl Malone

Ability may get you to the top, but it takes
character to keep you there.

John Wooden

Play to win, observe the rules,
and act like a gentleman.

Claire Bee

Size is not the measure of a man's worth,
unless you are talking about the size
of his heart.

Wilt Chamberlain

It's a battle of wills, not a battle of skills.

Isiah Thomas

Some criticism will be honest, some won't.
Some praise you will deserve, some you
won't. You can't let praise or criticism
get to you. It's a weakness to get
caught up in either one.

John Wooden

What you are as a person is far more
important than what you are
as a basketball player.

John Wooden

It's hard to learn when you win.

Bill Sharman

Accept a loss as a learning experience,
and never point fingers at your teammates.

Michael Jordan

A raggedy ride is better than a smooth one.

Nolan Richardson

The people who
barbecued me ran
out of sauce.

Nolan Richardson

To come back from a surgery and
walk properly again; to come back and get
50 points in a ball game again is something
I'm awfully proud of and will never forget.

Bernard King

Injuries are a learning experience.

Kareem Abdul-Jabbar

When I was young, my dad whupped me
into line. Thank God he did.

Shaquille O'Neal

As far as character-building goes, you build more character by winning than you do by losing.

Adolph Rupp

Never underestimate the heart of a champion.

Rudy Tomjanovich

12

Winning and Losing

The road to the Hall of Fame goes through the win column. In basketball, the formula for greatness is simple: Get into the championship tournament and win the last game.

Al McGuire tried to put things in perspective when he said, "Winning is overrated. The only time it's really important is in surgery and war." But his actions spoke louder than his words when Coach McGuire wept on the bench as his Marquette Warriors won the national title.

Basketball is a game of joy and heartbreak; often, the game is determined by a single shot. The game's greatest players are ever-anxious to take that final shot and accept the consequences. Like McGuire, they understand that basketball is not a matter of life and death. It only seems that way.

The Greek biographer Plutarch wrote, "Those who take aim at great deeds must suffer greatly." Had he been a basketball fan, Plutarch might have added that those who take aim at game-winning shots must also be willing to suffer. That's simply the price of greatness.

I know I have plenty of enemies, but I'd
  rather be the most hated winning coach in
the country than the most popular losing one.

Adolph Rupp

It's easy to stick together when you're
  winning. But the true test of a team
  is to stick together when you lose.

Dale Brown

Tough losses stay with you more
  than the wins.

Jerry West

The ones you can never get out of your mind
  are the ones you lose when
  you should have won.

Bill Walton

It's not the end of the world when you lose
a game, although sometimes as coaches,
we feel like it. There's more to
this game of life than this game.

Lenny Wilkens

Winning never gets old.

John Havlicek

Losing is as much a part of coaching as winning.

Ray Meyer

You know what
happiness is? In coaching,
happiness is winning
on the road.

Al McGuire

I didn't have a best move.
My best move was
just to win.

Magic Johnson

Remember that basketball is a game
of habits. If you make the other guy deviate
from his habits, you've got him.

Bill Russell

Winning basketball goes beyond
the superstar. The secret is balance,
teamwork, hustle, and defense.

Red Auerbach

Some people worry about statistics,
but I worry about winning.
Statistics are for losers.

Pete Maravich

Winning makes everyone a star.

Lenny Wilkens

My job is simple: Make my teammates
think win, win, win.

Penny Hardaway

After winning the championship game,
I remember a joy over the next 48 hours,
a spring of joy, a feeling of great
accomplishment. For 16 years
I had waited for that moment.

Elvin Hayes

The higher you climb, the more you feel
the disappointment when you don't reach
the top.

John Thompson

Becoming number one is easier
than staying number one.

Bill Bradley

The first time you win a championship, it's a honeymoon. The second time, it's an odyssey.

Phil Jackson

Defeat and failure are my enemies.

Adolph Rupp

I would not give one iota to make the trip
from cradle to the grave unless l could live
in a competitive world.

Adolph Rupp

Winning a championship is never easy.
And it shouldn't be.

Phil Jackson

Sometimes winning a basketball game is just plain luck.

Dean Smith

I don't want undue dejection when we lose
or any undue celebration when we win.

John Wooden

The taste of defeat has a richness
of experience all its own.

Bill Bradley

Victory is fraught with as much danger
as glory.

Bill Bradley

The only thing harder to handle
than winning too much is losing too much.

John Wooden

As you get older, you understand that winning has its place, and losing is not the end of the world.

Red Auerbach

The awards and championships are great, but the journey is what I'll remember.

Hakeem Olajuwon

13

Observations on Referees, The Fat Lady, and Other Facts Of Basketball Life

In 1989, Manute Bol was utilizing every inch of his 7'6" frame on America's hardwood courts. That year, Bol's Sudanese uncle sent a dire message from the homeland: "If Manute is still alive, tell him his wife has married another man and most of his cattle were stolen by Arab militia. If he needs any help, we're still here."

The following messages, while not as urgent as Bol's, may be equally as entertaining. Enjoy.

The game I invented in 1891 back at the Springfield, Massachusetts YMCA college has had a fine part in the development of better international understanding.

James Naismith

Basketball may have been invented in Massachusetts, but it was made for Indiana.

Bobby Knight

World War II is really the thing that spread basketball around the world. The soldiers played it.

Bob Kurland

The things that brought world competition together were jets and television.

Red Auerbach

It's a world game. It's not expensive to play. You can have fun playing by yourself or one-on-one with another person. Basketball is for everyone.

Red Auerbach

The invention of basketball was not an accident. It was developed to meet a need. Those boys simply would not play drop the handkerchief.

James Naismith

A referee has to encourage action on the court, not cripple it with technicalities.

Earl Strom

If you are a referee, you have no friends.

Charlie Eckman

A basketball referee has one of the few jobs in life where you're in charge, but you're supposed to be anonymous.

Earl Strom

For a basketball official,
the highest accolade
is silence.

Dolly Stark

They always take the good big guy ahead of the good little guy. That's the NBA way.

Sean Elliott

I don't think you can ever have enough big people.

Jimmy Rodgers

Quickness, not height, is probably the greatest attribute a team can have.

Jerry Tarkanian

Height is overrated.

Charles Barkley

People talk small but draft big.

Frank Catapano

Nothing instigates jealousy like winning.

Red Auerbach

Nobody roots for Goliath.

Wilt Chamberlain

When you're the top dog, everybody wants to put you in the pound.

Charles Barkley

I'd rather have
a lot of talent and
a little experience
than a little talent and
a lot of experience.

John Wooden

You don't play against opponents. You play against the game of basketball.

Bobby Knight

It's not so important who starts the game as who finishes it.

John Wooden

Leadership is getting others to believe in you.

Larry Bird

Basketball is a game easy to play and difficult to master.

James Naismith

It's what you learn
after you know it all
that counts.

John Wooden

Ego is a paradox — it is the point from which you see, but it can also make you blind.

Bill Russell

Defense can be taught.
Offense is something different. Offense is something you're born with.

Red Auerbach

It's better to say you won the championship game than you played in it.

Bobby Knight

If you could bottle all the emotion in a basketball game, you'd have enough hate to start a war and enough joy to stop one.

Bill Russell

A lack of success doesn't necessarily mean it's someone else's fault.

Bill Walton

NBA stands for No Babies Allowed.

Charles Barkley

Whenever you lose, there's going to be criticism. That's why they invented talk radio.

Rudy Tomjanovich

I don't think about my dunk shots. I just have to make sure I have a place to land.

Julius Erving

Minor surgery is when they do the operation on someone else.

Bill Walton

As a kid, I had a vivid imagination in the back yard. I was player, coach, announcer, even timekeeper. And if I missed the last shot at the buzzer, there was always time for one more — or ten.

Jerry West

I wish all players had an opportunity to play in the championship for the Lakers or the Celtics during my time. Then, they'd understand what basketball really is.

Magic Johnson

Basketball is sharing.

Phil Jackson

Basketball has been a powerful force for understanding and race relations in our society.

John McLendon, Jr.

Even when I'm old and gray, I won't be able to play it, but I'll still love the game.

Michael Jordan

It ain't over till the fat lady sings.

Dick Motta's Favorite Motto

Basketball, finally, is a popular spectator's game. How many millions the world over gather to cheer their favorite teams is beyond guess.

James Naismith, 1939

People say, "Relax, the game is over. The game is over." Well, the game is never over.

Red Auerbach

Sources

Sources

Kareem Abdul-Jabbar 29, 64, 81, 92, 128
Phog Allen 101, 105
Red Auerbach 20, 30, 32, 46, 52, 63, 64, 67, 73, 89, 97,
    109, 112, 115, 117, 137, 143, 146, 152, 156, 160
Charles Barkley 43, 77, 87, 88, 103, 150, 152, 157
Claire Bee 74, 108, 125
Larry Bird 23, 28, 33, 38, 54, 55, 59, 60, 80, 88, 92, 120,
    154
Bill Bradley 138, 142
Dale Brown 19, 36, 107, 121, 132
Larry Brown 102
John Bunn 107
John Calipari 27, 46, 89
Frank Catapano 151
Wilt Chamberlain 80, 84, 125, 152
John Chaney 26, 47
Bob Cousy 23, 115
Dave Cowens 34
Chuck Daly 15, 49, 68, 97, 114, 116
Dave DeBusschere 72
Charlie Eckman 148
Sean Elliott 150
Julius Erving 30, 42, 77, 120, 157
Patrick Ewing 64
Bill Fitch 76
Jack Givens 90
Luther Gulick 119
Bob Hansen 102
Penny Hardaway 138
John Havlicek 58, 133
Elvin Hayes 35, 138
Grant Hill 48, 80
Hank Iba 18, 37, 42, 61, 114

About the Author

Criswell Freeman is a Doctor of Clinical Psychology living in Nashville, Tennessee. He is the author of *When Life Throws You a Curveball, Hit It* and *The Wisdom Series* from WALNUT GROVE PRESS. He is also a published and recorded country music songwriter.

About Wisdom Books

Wisdom Books chronicle memorable quotations in an easy-to-read style. Written by Criswell Freeman, this series provides inspiring, thoughtful and humorous messages from entertainers, athletes, scientists, politicians, clerics, writers and renegades. Each title focuses on a particular region or special interest.

Combining his passion for quotations with extensive training in psychology, Dr. Freeman revisits timeless themes such as perseverance, courage, love, forgiveness and faith.

"Quotations help us remember the simple yet profound truths that give life perspective and meaning," notes Freeman. "When it comes to life's most important lessons, we can all use gentle reminders."

The Wisdom Series

by Dr. Criswell Freeman

Regional Titles

Wisdom Made In America	ISBN 1-887655-07-7
The Book of Southern Wisdom	ISBN 0-9640955-3-X
The Wisdom of the Midwest	ISBN 1-887655-17-4
The Wisdom of the West	ISBN 1-887655-31-X
The Book of Texas Wisdom	ISBN 0-9640955-8-0
The Book of Florida Wisdom	ISBN 0-9640955-9-9
The Book of California Wisdom	ISBN 1-887655-14-X
The Book of New York Wisdom	ISBN 1-887655-16-6
The Book of New England Wisdom	ISBN 1-887655-15-8

Sports Titles

The Golfer's Book of Wisdom	ISBN 0-9640955-6-4
The Wisdom of Southern Football	ISBN 0-9640955-7-2
The Book of Stock Car Wisdom	ISBN 1-887655-12-3
The Wisdom of Old-Time Baseball	ISBN 1-887655-08-5
The Book of Football Wisdom	ISBN 1-887655-18-2
The Book of Basketball Wisdom	ISBN 1-887655-32-8
The Fisherman's Guide to Life	ISBN 1-887655-30-1

Special Interest Titles

The Book of Country Music Wisdom	ISBN 0-9640955-1-3
The Wisdom of Old-Time Television	ISBN 1-887655-64-6